Civil Elegies
and Other Poems

By the same author

Civil Elegies
and Other Poems

Dennis Lee

Anansi
Toronto
1972

An earlier version of *Civil Elegies* appeared in 1968.

The author wishes to thank the Canada Council for its assistance during the writing of this book. The Council also aided with its publication.

Cover design by Hilary Norman
Photo·by Graeme Gibson

Printed in Canada by The Hunter Rose Company

ISBN: 0 88784 023 X (paper); 0 88784 123 6 (cloth)

   3 4 5   76 75

House of Anansi Press

Contents

I

COMING BACK

Illisque pro annis uxore

400: Coming Home

You are still on the highway and the great light of
noon comes over the asphalt, the gravelled
shoulders. You are on the highway, there is a kind of
laughter, the cars pound
south. Over your shoulder the scrub-grass, the fences,
the fields wait patiently as though someone
believed in them. The light has laid it
upon them. One
crow scrawks. The edges
take care of themselves, there is
no strain, you can almost hear it, you
inhabit it.

Back in the city many things you lived for
are coming apart.
Transistor rock still fills
back yards, in the parks young men do things to
hondas; there will be
heat lightning, beer on the porches, goings on.
That is not it.

And you are still on the highway. There are no
houses, no farms. Across the median, past the swish and thud of the
northbound cars, beyond the opposite
fences, the fields, the
climbing escarpment, solitary in the
bright eye of the sun the
birches dance, and they
dance. They have
their reasons. You do not know
anything.
Cicadas call now, in the darkening swollen air there is dust
in your nostrils; a
kind of laughter; you are still on the highway.

Glad for the Wrong Reasons

Night and day it
goes on, it goes
on. I hear what feel like ponderous immaculate
lizards moving through; I call it
absence I call it silence but often I am
glad for the wrong reasons.
Many times at 6:00 a.m. there is a
fiendish din of cans, like now
for instance and we
lunge up punctured through the
blur & the broken
glass of last night's argument, fetching up
groggy on a landscape of bed, well I can
taste our dubious breath and look it's
me, babe, I wabble my neck and lounge the
trophy from my dream across your belly, your
body slouches towards me, jesus, there is
something about our lives that
doesn't make sense, tomorrow
I'll fix them up, remind me, the garbage
cans have stopped now but the room is
bright too bright to
fix I mean ah jesus I burrow slow
motion back to sleep; and the
lizards resume their
phosphorescent progress, I crowd towards them but I should
not be here now, swallowing fast & doggedly gawking &
staying put and glad but glad for the wrong reasons.

Brunswick Avenue

We are in
bed, the dark is close to my face. Hilary
moans in the crib. It is getting
warm in here, the covers are
close, I am going
into it.

All the long-legged suns have clotted again
in my head, and only keyholes know a song.
Emptiness is my alibi, but it is pitted with syllables like
caterpillars moving hoarsely across the face of the Bible.

Outside, the rasp of a snow-shovel
grates in the dark.
Lovely
sound, I hang onto it. In the
stillness I feel the flakes and the heft of
that man's left arm, and the sudden
twinge as the shovel lets go of the wet snow I am going into it

Many spaces no longer belong to the ones who once filled them.
The air keeps striding through.
Pinholes arrive & open like sprayguns, and always
the long-legged suns are combining.

Beside me on the bed the woman with whom I did
great violence for years, preserving
dalliance and stigmata, stretches
easy in her after-pleasure, sleeping.
Clothes and our wetness load the air.
Her hair is on my shoulder.
The covers lift and fold, and the shovel scrapes and I hear the
endless holes in the night hang down and the snow and our fragile breathing.

He Asks Her

What kind of
    pickle were we in? Every
piddling triumph I dragged into the house—
                            by the ears
    ("I fixed the washer in the outside tap.")
by the snout
    ("I sold another book today. That makes eleven.")
or by the curly Q of its little pink tale
    ("I seduced Madame Nhu this aft. In the john at Eglinton station.")
                —they all became weapons in the stockpile
Sometimes I trickled under the door to tell you
    sometimes I walked thru the wall, all shucks & left-handed
sometimes I'd bound in via the second-storey window, hanging by my
    canine incisors.
But what kind of
    pickle were we in? You had to
turn and finger the miserable little feat,
    testing the cutting edge on your own flesh,
and I would savour the way something
                closed inside me and fondled itself,
knowing that soon you'd be
    cast down again, that I would be rejected.

High Park, by Grenadier Pond

Whatever I say, lady
it is not that
I say our lives are working—but feel the
ambush of soft air—, nor that our
rancour & precious remorse can be
surrendered merely because the earth has taken
green dominion here, beneath us
the belly of grass is real; and lady
it is not that
lovers by the score come sporting
fantasies like we had   strolling
bright-eyed past the portulaca—we could
whisper messages, they would be
snarls in our own blood;
and I am
bitter about our reconciliations, we panicked, we
snowed ourselves each time. So lady
it is not that
I hanker for new beginnings—confession and
copout, we know that game, it's as real as the
whiskey, the fights, the pills.
And I do not start this now because the grass is green,
and not because in front of us the
path makes stately patterns down the slope to Grenadier and all the
random ambling of the couples hangs
like courtly bygones in the shining air;
the old longing is there, it always will but I will not
allow it.

But there is
you, lady.   I
want you to
be, and I want you.
Lie here on the grass beside me,
hear me tie my tongue in knots.

I can't talk brave palaver like
         I did 10 years ago—I
       used up all the words—but now I
sense my centre in these new
       gropings, wary, near yours lady,
         coming to
              difficult sanities.
     I want to be here.

The Morning of the Second Day: He Tells Her

How will you handle my body?
What will I do to your name?
New selves kept tramping through me like a
herd of signatures, I mislaid
sentences halfway, the trademark was *ummm* . . . ?
Which one of me did you want?

Hey but that was another life, and donning the
one-way flesh, now glad and
half at home at last in the set of your neck,
the carriage of your thighs, I believe I sense
the difficult singularity of the man I
am not ready for.

But how will you handle my body?
Some day ten years from now we'll both
wake up, and stretch, and stare at somebody's ceiling—
our own, sweet jesus our *very own ceiling!*—and boggle, with
ten-year thoughts in mind.
Look out, I believe we're married & lap your
hair across my face, this must make sense but what will I
do to your beautiful name?

Recollection

I remember still
     a gentle girl, just married, how she
drew her husband down, they had
     no practice but she gave him warm
openings till he became a
     cocky simpleton inside her,
coming like kingdom come for the excellent
     pleasure it made in her body.

When It Is Over

The low-light recedes, the records recede, skin
        empties. Under my eyes
your eyes recede, I brush your cheek you feel what
        touch what clumsy much-loved man
receding? Your body is full of listening,
        exquisite among its own
shockwaves.   So. What
        space are you going into?

Over & over, love, what other
        music? Your
eyelids will be here for
        centuries, do not come to.
But flicker, come deeper, let be—the jubilation
        eases through your
body.   So. What
        space have you gone into?

Slowly, love, beneath me
        your breathing returns.
Now it is over, the flesh and resonance that filled that
        other space do not come to and
try to tell me where, for it is over.
        But drowse off now; as the after-pleasure settles
gently into our lives, it is over and
        over, and over, and over, and over and over.

Night

Night one more time, the darkness
close out there on the snow.
Goddamn war, goddamn smog, close the blind.

How many times have you
stared through that window at darkness?
Come on over here, lie on top of me, let's fuck.

Good men would think twice
about it, they would
not be born in this century.

Night one more time, great
lobotomy. Come on over here with your body, lie down, tomorrow
it all starts again.

In A Bad Time

So much is gone now, bright and suicidal,
so much is on the verge.

What good are words among the
rock, the glittering wreckage?

Fallout falls; the empires breed
the nightmares that they need.

The only words are lives.
Friend.   Friend.

Thursday

Powerful men can fuck up too. It is Thursday,
a mean old lady has died, she got him his
paper route and there is still that whiff of
ju-jube and doilies from her front hall; a stroke; he can
taste them going soggy; some in his pocket too, they always picked up
lint; anyway, she is dead.
And tonight there are things to do in the study, he has a
report, he has the kids, it is
almost too much. Forty-five years, and
still the point eludes him whenever he stops to think.
Next morning,
hacking the day into shape on the phone, there is still no
way—routine & the small ache,
he cannot accommodate both.
At Hallowe'en too, in her hall.
And I know which one he takes and that
night at six, while the kids are tackling his legs with their small tussling,
how he fends them off, tells them "Play upstairs"; one day
they will be dead also with their jelly beans.
In her kitchen, she had a parrot that said "Down the hatch!"

More Claiming

That one is me too—belting thru
   school to the rhythms of glory, tripping,
      blinking at vanishing place-names
    Etobicoke Muskoka Labrador then Notting Hill Gate but he could
     never keep them straight,
  though as they ran together they always had
    people in them, like ketchup on his shirt.
Extra-gang spikers and singalong, I believe that was
    Labrador? Teachers. That
girl in Stockholm—Christ! what did they
    expect? the man was otherwise engaged.

For there were treks, attacks and
    tribal migrations of meaning, wow
careening thru his skull, the doves &
    dodos that descended, scary
partnerships with God, new selves erupting
    messianic daily—all the grand
adrenalin parade!
    He was supposed to wear matching socks?

It was a messy pubescent
    surfeit of selves but there were
three I didn't know about,
    the sabotage kids.
They never budged.
One was perpetually leaving his
    penis behind in garbage bags. One had a
bazooka stuck in his throat, hence had some
    difficulty speaking.
The third would sob all night in the lonesome night,
    crying for something damp, and close, and warm.

I came across them far too late.
   They kept on dousing
     epiphanies, misdirecting traffic.
   They kept on daring me to
    break down, like a carburetor with a passion for wildflowers.

Heaven and Earth

Ordinary   moving
  stoplight & manhole
   maple tree   birch tree   oak
dandelions   crabgrass
   ferry boats   Andromeda
   fathers   and mothers, and

heaven and earth and all
   vivacious things that
   throng around a man
will not approach until he
   hears himself pronounce "I
   hate you" with his body.

Sibelius Park

I

Walking north from his other lives in a fine rain
        through the high-rise pavilion on Walmer
   lost in the vague turbulence he harbours
        Rochdale   Anansi   how many
     routine wipeouts has he performed since he was born?
                     and mostly himself;
          drifting north to the three-storey
   turrets & gables, the squiggles and arches and
  baleful asymmetric glare of the houses he loves
          Toronto gothic
walking north in the fine rain, going home through the late afternoon
  he comes to Sibelius Park.
Across that green expanse he sees
     the cars parked close, every second licence yankee, he thinks of
  the war and the young men dodging, his wife inside
    with her counsel, her second thoughts
          and the children, needing more than they can give;
and behind him, five blocks south, his other lives
   in rainy limbo till tomorrow
      Rochdale, yes   Anansi
       the fine iconic books, sheepish errata
         shitwork in a cold basement, moody
       triumphs of the mind
             hassling printers   hassling banks
     and the grim dudgeon with friends—men with
  deep combative egos, ridden men, they cannot sit still, they go on
            brooding on Mao   on Gandhi
and they cannot resolve their lives but together they make up
            emblems of a unified civilization,
     the fine iconic books;
               he is rooted in books & in
  that other place, where icons come alive among the faulty
        heroes & copouts, groping for some new tension of
    mind and life, casting the type in their own
     warm flesh
         hassling builders   hassling banks

and he is constantly coming and going away, appalled by the force of
              wishful affirmations, he thinks of the war, he
hears himself 10 years ago affirming his faith in Christ
        in the lockers, still half-clasped in pads & a furtive
           virgin still, flailing the
lukewarm school with rumours of God, gunning for psychic opponents
    though he could not hit his father and what broke at last was the
       holiness; and he can't go back there any more
  without hearing the livelong flourish
          of Christ in his mouth, always he tasted His funny
taste in every arraignment but it was himself he was burying.
And the same struggle goes on and when
             he drinks too much, or cannot sleep for his body's
      jaundiced repose he can scarcely read a word he wrote,
        though the words are just but his work has
    the funny taste and his life pulls back and snickers when he begins.

And then Sibelius Park!
      The grass is wet, it
  gleams, across the park's wide
      vista the lanes of ornamental
  shrub come breathing and the sun is filling the
      rinsed air till the green goes luminous and it does it
                  does, it comes clear.

II

Supper is over, I sit
      holed up in my study. I have no
answers again and I do not trust the
      simplicities, nor Sibelius Park;
                I am not to be trusted with them.

But I rest in one thing. The play of
      dusk and atmospherics, the beautiful rites of
synthaesthesia, are not to be believed;
      but that grisly counter-presence, the warfare in the lockers, myself
against myself, the years of desperate affirmation and the dank
      manholes of ego which stink when they
come free at last
    —the seamy underside of every stiff
iconic self—which are hard   which are welcome
are no more real than that unreal man who stood and took them in;
      are no more real than the fake epiphanies,
              though they ache to bring them down.

For they are all given, they are not
      to be believed but constantly
they are being
      given, moment by moment, the icons and what they
suppress, here and
      here and though they are not real they have their own real
presence, like a mirror in the grass and in the
      bodies we live in we are
acceptable.

There is nothing to be afraid of.

Coming Back

Saying crabgrass, plantain, begonia,
saying Queen Anne's lace, devil's paint-brush, flag.

Time I was young I thought
letting them go was holy.

Quartz, saying granite, saying dirt-farm, outcrop,
limestone, fossil, saying shale.

Coming back who needs it—giving up the
things I never owned?

Saying city, chevvy, collision the sirens;
hungry, saying finger, saying food.

Words for the Given

If I take up space in the silence, master, friend—
let it be, we all live here and do not matter.

So I did my shabby trick again; we
both saw it happen, I won't get away with it.

And nothing is enough.   I did not say that
for content, it was a greeting.

No listen, I still don't know but what does that
matter? Listen.   It is.   It is.   It is.

II

CIVIL ELEGIES

Pro patria

Man is by nature a political animal, and to know
that citizenship is an impossibility is to be cut
off from one of the highest forms of life.

George Grant

Do not cling to the notion of emptiness;
Consider all things alike. My friend,
There is only one word that I know now
And I do not know its name.

Saraha

1

Often I sit in the sun and brooding over the city, always
in airborne shapes among the pollution I hear them, returning;
pouring across the square
in fetid descent, they darken the towers
and the wind-swept place of meeting and whenever
the thick air clogs my breathing it teems with their presence.
Many were born in Canada, and living unlived lives they died
of course but died truncated, stunted, never at
home in native space and not yet
citizens of a human body of kind. And it is Canada
that specialized in this deprivation. Therefore the spectres arrive, congregating
    in bitter droves, thick in the April sunlight,
accusing us and we are no different, though you would not expect
the furies assembled in hogtown and ring me round, invisible, demanding
what time of our lives we wait for till we shall start to be.
Until they come the wide square stretches out
serene and singly by moments it takes us in, each one for now
a passionate civil man, until it
sends us back to the acres of gutted intentions,
back to the concrete debris, to parking scars and the four-square tiers
of squat and righteous lives. And here
once more, I watch the homing furies' arrival.

I sat one morning by the Moore, off to the west
ten yards and saw though diffident my city nailed against the sky
in ordinary glory.
It is not much to ask. A place, a making,
two towers, a teeming, a genesis, a city.
And the men and women moved in their own space,
performing their daily lives, and their presence occurred
in time as it occurred, patricians in
muddy York and made their compact together against the gangs of the new.
And as that crumpled before the shambling onset, again the
lives we had not lived in phalanx invisibly staining
the square and vistas, casting back I saw
regeneration twirl its blood and the rebels riding

riderless down Yonge Street, plain men much
goaded by privilege—our other origin, and cried
"Mackenzie knows a word, Mackenzie
knows a meaning!" but it was not true. Eight hundred-odd steely Canadians
turned tail at the cabbage patch when a couple of bullets fizzed
and the loyalists, scared skinny by the sound of their own gunfire,
gawked and bolted south to the fort like rabbits,
the rebels for their part bolting north to the pub: the first
spontaneous mutual retreat in the history of warfare.
Canadians, in flight.

Buildings oppress me, and the sky-concealing wires
bunch zigzag through the air. I know
the dead persist in
buildings, by-laws, porticos—the city I live in
is clogged with their presence; they
dawdle about in our lives and form a destiny, still
incomplete, still dead weight, still
demanding whether Canada will be.

But the mad bomber, Chartier of Major Street, Chartier
said it: that if a country has no past,
neither is it a country and promptly
blew himself to bits in the parliament john, leaving as civil testament
assorted chunks of prophet, twitching and
bobbing to rest in the flush.
And what can anyone do in this country, baffled and
making our penance for ancestors, what did they leave us? Indian-swindlers,
stewards of unclaimed earth and rootless what does it matter if they, our
forebears' flesh and bone were often
good men, good men do not matter to history.
And what can we do here now, for at last we have no notion
of what we might have come to be in America, alternative, and how make public
a presence which is not sold out utterly to the modern? utterly? to the
savage inflictions of what is for real, it pays off, it is only
accidentally less than human?

In the city I long for, green trees still
asphyxiate. The crowds emerge at five from jobs
that rankle and lag. Heavy developers
pay off aldermen still; the craft of neighbourhood,
its whichway streets and generations
anger the planners, they go on jamming their maps
with asphalt panaceas; single men
still eke out evenings courting, in parks, alone.
A man could spend a lifetime looking for
peace in that city. And the lives give way around him—marriages
founder, the neighbourhoods sag—until
the emptiness comes down on him to stay.
But in the city I long for men complete
their origins. Among the tangle of
hydro, hydrants, second mortgages, amid
the itch for new debentures, greater expressways,
in sober alarm they jam their works of progress, asking where in truth
they come from and to whom they must belong.
And thus they clear a space in which
the full desires of those that begot them, great animating desires
that shrank and grew hectic as the land pre-empted their lives
might still take root, which eddy now and
drift in the square, being neither alive nor dead.
And the people accept a flawed inheritance
and they give it a place in their midst, forfeiting progress, forfeiting
dollars, forfeiting yankee visions of cities that in time it might grow
whole at last in their lives, they might
belong once more to their forebears, becoming their own men.

To be our own men! in dread to live
the land, our own harsh country, beloved, the prairie, the foothills—
and for me it is lake by rapids by stream-fed lake, threading
north through the terminal vistas of black spruce, in a
bitter, cherished land it is farm after
farm in the waste of the continental outcrop—
for me it is Shield but wherever terrain informs our lives and claims us;

and then, no longer haunted by
unlived presence, to live the cities:
to furnish, out of the traffic and smog and the shambles of dead precursors,
a civil habitation that is
human, and our own.

The spectres drift across the square in rows.
How empire permeates! And we sit down
in Nathan Phillips Square, among the sun,
as if our lives were real.
Lacunae. Parking lots. Regenerations.
Newsstand euphorics and Revell's sign, that not
one countryman has learned, that
men and women live that
they may make that
life worth dying. Living. Hey,
the dead ones! Gentlemen, generations of
acquiescent spectres gawk at the chrome
on American cars on Queen Street, gawk and slump and retreat.
And over the square where I sit, congregating above the Archer
they crowd in a dense baffled throng and the sun does not shine through.

2

Master and Lord, where
are you?
A man moves back and forth
between what must be done to save the world
and what will save his soul,
and neither is real. For many years
I could not speak your name, nor now but
even stilled at times by openings like
joy my whole life
aches, the streets I walk along to work declare
your absence, the headlines
declare it, the nation, and
over and over the harried lives I
watch and live with, holding my breath and
sometimes a thing rings true—
they all give way and declare your real absence.

Master and Lord,
let be. I can say
nothing about you that does not
vanish like tapwater.
I know
the world is not enough; a woman straightens
and turns from the sink and asks her life the
question, why should she
fake it? and after a moment she
shrugs, and returns to the sink. A man's
adrenalin takes hold, at a meeting he makes
his point, and pushes and sees that
things will happen now . . . and then in the pause he knows
there are endless things in the world and this is not for real.

Whatever is lovely, whatever deserves
contempt, whatever dies—
over and over, in every thing we meet
we meet that emptiness.

It is a homecoming, as men once knew
their lives took place in you.
And we cannot get on, no matter how we
rearrange our lives and we cannot let go for
then there is nothing at all.

Master and Lord, there was a
measure once.
There was a time when men could say
my life, my job, my home
and still feel clean.
The poets spoke of earth and heaven. There were no symbols.

3

The light rides easy on people dozing at noon in Toronto, or
here it does, in the square, with the white spray hanging
upward in plumes on the face of the pool, and the kids, and the thrum of the
    traffic,
and the people come and they feel no consternation, dozing at
lunchtime; even the towers comply.
And they prevail in their placid continuance, idly unwrapping their food
day after day on the slabs by the pool, warm in the summer sun.
Day after day the light rides easy.
Nothing is important.
But once at noon I felt my body's pulse contract and
balk in the space of the square, it puckered and jammed till nothing
worked, and casting back and forth
the only resonance that held was in the Archer.
Great bronze simplicity, that muscled form
was adequate in the aimless expanse—it held, and tense and
waiting to the south I stood until the
clangor in my forearms found its outlet.
And when it came I knew that stark heraldic form is not
great art; for it is real, great art is less than its necessity.
But it held, when the monumental space of the square
went slack, it moved in sterner space.
Was shaped by earlier space and it ripples with
wrenched stress, the bronze is flexed by
blind aeonic throes
that bred and met in slow enormous impact,
and they are still at large for the force in the bronze churns
through it, and lunges beyond and also the Archer declares
that space is primal, raw, beyond control and drives toward a
living stillness, its own.
But if some man by the pool, doing his workaday
job in the city, tangled in other men's
futures with ticker-tape, hammering
type for credits or bread, or in for the day, wiped out in Long Branch
by the indelible sting of household acts of war,
or whatever; if a man strays into that

vast barbaric space it happens that he enters into
void and will go
under, or he must himself become void.

We live on occupied soil.
Across the barren Shield, immortal scrubland and our own,
where near the beginning the spasms of lava
settled to bedrock schist,
barbaric land, initial, our
own, scoured bare under
crush of the glacial recessions
and later it broke the settlers, towing them
deeper and deeper each year beneath the
gritty sprinkle of soil, till men who had worked their farms for a lifetime
could snap in a month from simple cessation of will,
though the brute surroundings went on—the flagrant changes
of maple and sumach, the water in ripples of light,
the faces of outcrop, the stillness, and up the slopes
a vast incessant green that drew the mind
beyond its tether, north, to muskeg and
stunted hackmatack, and then the whine of icy tundra north to the pole—
despotic land, inhuman yet
our *own,* where else on earth? and reaping stone
from the bush their fathers cleared, the sons gave
way and they drank all year, or went strange, or they sat and stared outside
as their cars settled back to slag and now what
races toward us on asphalt across the Shield—
by truck, by TV minds and the ore-bearing flatcars—
is torn from the land and the mute oblivion of
all those fruitless lives, it no longer
stays for us, immemorial adversary, but is shipped and
divvied abroad though wrested whole from the Shield.

Take Tom Thomson, painter; he
did his work in the Shield.
Could guide with a blindfold on. Was part of the bush. Often when night

40

came down in a subtle rush and the scorched scrub still
ached for miles from the fires he paddled direct through
the palpable dark, hearing only the push and
drip of the blade for hours and then very suddenly the radiance of the
renewed land broke over his canvas. So. It was his
job. But no two moments land with the same sideswipe
and Thomson, for all his savvy, is very damp and
trundled by submarine currents, pecked by the fish out
somewhere cold in the Shield and the far loons percolate
high in November and he is not painting their cry.

Small things ignite us, and the quirky particulars
flare on all sides.
A cluster of birches, in moonlight;
a jack pine, gnarled and
focussing heaven and earth—
these might fend off void.
Or under the poolside arches the sunlight, skidding on paper destroyers,
kindles a dazzle, skewing the sense. Like that. Any
combination of men and time can start the momentary
ignition. If only it were enough.
But it is two thousand years since Christ's carcass rose in a glory,
and now the shiny ascent is not for us, Thomson is
done and we cannot
malinger among the bygone acts of grace. For
many are called but none are chosen now, we are the evidence
for downward momentum, although despite our longing still restrained
within the real, as Thomson's body really did
decay and vying to praise him we
bicker about which grave the carcass fills.

New silences occur in the drone of the square's great spaces.
The light overbalances, shadows
appear, the people walk away.
But massy and knotted and still the Archer continues its space,
which violates our lives, and reminds us, and has no mercy upon us.

For a people which lays its whiskey and violent machines
on a land that is primal, and native, which takes that land in greedy
innocence but will not live it, which is not claimed by its own
and sells that land off even before it has owned it,
traducing the immemorial pacts of men and earth, free and
beyond them, exempt by miracle from the fate of the race—
that people will botch its cities, its greatest squares
will scoff at its money and stature, and prising wide
a civil space to live in, by the grace of its own invention it will
fill that space with the artifacts of death.

On Queen Street, therefore, in Long Branch, wherever the
people have come upon it, say that the
news is as bad as we thought:
we have spent the bankroll; here, in this place,
it is time to honour the void.

4

Among the things which
hesitate to be, is void our
vocation? The houses on the street
hold back from us, across the welter of city blocks
our friendships keep stalling,
even the square falls away and the acts of our statesmen
will not come real though we long for it.
Dwelling among the
bruised and infinitely binding world
are we not meant to
relinquish it all, to begin at last
the one abundant psalm of letting be?

If only it
held. If only
here and now were not fastened so
deep in the flesh and goodbye, but how should a man
alive and tied to the wreckage that surrounds him,
the poisoned air goodbye, goodbye the lakes,
the earth and precious habitat of species,
goodbye the grainy sense of place, worn down in
words and the local ways of peoples, goodbye the children returning
as strangers to their roots and generations,
and cities dying of concrete, city goodbye my city of passionate bickering
neighbourhoods the corner stores
all ghosts among the high-rise, like bewildered nations after their
surrender as their boundaries
diminish to formalities on maps goodbye, so many
lives gone down the drain in the service of empire,
bombing its demon opponents though they bleed like men, goodbye
and not that all things die but that they die meanly, and
goodbye the lull of the sun in the square, goodbye and
goodbye the magisterial life of the mind, in the domination of number every
excellent workaday thing all spirited
men and women ceaselessly jammed at their breaking
points goodbye who have such little time on earth and constantly fastened
how should a man stop caring?

And yet the death of lakes, the gutting of our self-respect,
even the passage of Canada—
these do not intrude such radical
bereavement merely to
humour us, to bid us declare
how painfully each passing brings us down.
Every thing we own will
disappear; nothing
belongs to us, and
only that nothing is home.
And this is what the things were telling us: if we can
face the rigours of detachment, meaning our
life, our job, our home, permitting it to
break over us, letting it
bring us down till every
itch and twitch of attachment loses its purchase,
at the dead-end of desire and for some it will last
a month and for some ten years, at last we
find ourselves in the midst of what abounds,
though that is not it but now we are set
free to cherish the world which has been stripped away by stages, and with no
reason the things are renewed: the people, Toronto, the elms
still greening in their blighted silhouettes—some dead some
burgeoning but none our property, and now they
move at last in the clearness of open space, within the
emptiness they move very cleanly in the vehement enjoyment of their bodies.

But what good is that in a nation of
losers and quislings? and for the few tenacious
citizens of a land that was never their own, watching the
ore and the oil and the shore-lines gutted
for dollars by men from abroad, watching Canadians
peddle their birthright and for these others, good
stateless men and women and may they go down in civil fury—
how should they clutch and fumble after beatitude, crouching for
years till emptiness renews an elm-tree,

and meanwhile the country is gone?
   I think much now of Garneau, master of emptiness,
who in the crowded streets of Montreal
saw not lost souls but a company of lost bodies, and
moving into himself gave thanks when he discovered
nothing but desert and void.
And I know that appetite in my own life,
at work, at home, in the square, and more insistent every day it presses
outward through the living will of the body,
straining to reach its ground, oblivion.
   But some face exile at home and sniping at corporations,
manic at times, and the patsies of empire their leaders lying for votes
till the impotence spreads in their veins, there is
shame abounding and sometimes a few good
gestures between the asphalt and sky that might have been adequate
once, and finally dying on occupied soil.
   Yet still they take the world full force on their nerve ends, leaving the
bloody impress of their bodies face forward in time and I believe
they will not go under until they have taken the measure of empire.

5

It would be better maybe if we could stop loving the children
and their delicate brawls, pelting across the square in tandem, deking
from cover to cover in raucous celebration and they are never
winded, bemusing us with the rites of our own
gone childhood; if only they stopped
mattering, the children, it might be possible, now
while the square lies stunned by noon.
What is real is fitful, and always the beautiful footholds
crumble the moment I set my mind aside, though the world does recur.
Better, I think, to avoid the scandal of being—the headlong particulars
which as they lose their animal purchase
cease to endorse us, though the ignominious hankering
goes on; this awakens the ache of being, and the lonesome ego
sets out once again dragging its lethal desires across the world,
which does not regard them.
Perhaps we should
bless what doesn't attach us, though I do not know
where we are to find nourishment.
So, in the square, it is a
blessed humdrum; the kids climb over the Archer, and
the pool reflects the sky, and the people passing by,
who doze, and gently from above the visible pollutants descend,
coating the towers' sheath. Sometimes it
works but once in summer looking up I saw the noxious cloud suspended
taut above the city, clenched, as now everywhere it is the
imperial way of life that bestows its fallout. And it did not
stay inert, but across the fabled horizon of Bay Street they came riding,
the liberators, the deputies of Jesus, the Marines, and had released
bacterial missiles over the Golden Horseshoe for love of all mankind,
and I saw my people streaming after calling welcome for the small change,
and I ran in my mind crying humiliation upon the country, as now I do also
    for it is
hard to stay at the centre when you're losing it one more time,
although the pool
reflects the placid sky, and the people passing by, and daily
our acquiescence presses down on us from above and we have no room to be.
It is the children's fault as they swarm for we cannot stop caring.

In a bad time, people, from an outpost of empire I write
bewildered, though on about living. It is to set down a nation's
failure of nerve; I mean complicity, which is signified by the
gaseous stain above us. For a man who
fries the skin of kids with burning jelly is a
criminal. Even though he loves children he is a criminal. Even though his
money pumps your oil he is criminal, and though his programs infest the air
   you breathe he is
criminal and though his honest quislings run your
government he is criminal and though you do not love his enemies he is
criminal and though you lose your job on his say-so he is criminal and
though your country will founder without him he is criminal and though he has
transformed the categories of your refusal by the pressure of his media he
   is a criminal.
And the consenting citizens of a minor and docile colony
are cogs in a useful tool, though in no way
necessary and scarcely
criminal at all and their leaders are
honourable men, as for example Paul Martin.

In Germany, the civic square in many little towns is
hallowed for people. Laid out just so, with
flowers and fountains and during the war you could come and
relax for an hour, catch a parade or just
get away from the interminable racket of the trains, clattering through the
outskirts with their lousy expendable cargo.
Little cafes often, fronting the square. Beer and a chance to relax.
And except for the children it's peaceful here
too, under the sun's warm sedation.

The humiliations of imperial necessity
are an old story, though it does not
improve in the telling and no man
believes it of himself.
Why bring up genocide? Why bring up
acquiescence, profiteering? Why bring up, again,

the deft emasculation of a country by the Liberal party of Canada?
It was not Mr Martin who sprayed the poison mist
on the fields of the Vietnamese, not in person nor fried civilians—he was
no worse a man than the other sellouts of history:
the Britons who went over to the legionaries, sadly for the sake of the
     larger peace,
the tired professors of Freiburg, Berlin, the statesmen at Munich, those
estimable men, and the lovers of peace, the brisk switchers who
told it in Budapest. Doesn't the
service of quiet diplomacy require dirty hands?
(Does the sun in summer pour its warm light into the square
for us to ignore?)
And then if it doesn't work one is finally
on the winning side—though that is
unkind: Mr Martin was an honourable man, as we are all
Canadians and honourable men.

And this is void, to participate in an
abomination larger than yourself. It is to fashion
other men's napalm and know it, to be a
Canadian safe in the square and watch the children dance and
dance and smell the lissome burning
bodies to be born in
old necessity to breathe polluted air and
come of age in Canada with lies and vertical on earth no man has drawn a
breath that was not lethal to some brother it is
yank and gook and hogtown linked in
guilty genesis it is the sorry mortal
sellout burning kids by proxy acquiescent
still though still denying it is merely to be human.

6

I am one for whom the world is constantly proving too much—
not this nor that, but the continental drift to barbarian
normalcy frightens me, I am constantly
stiffening before my other foot touches the ground and numb in my
stance I hear the country pouring on past me gladly on all sides,
towed and protesting but pelting very fast downhill,
and though I do not decry technopolis I can see only the bread and circuses
    to come,
and no man will use a mirror to shave, in case he
glimpse himself and abroad there will come obscenity, a senseless procession
    of holy wars
and we will carry the napalm for our side, proud of our clean hands.
I can't converse with friends without discussing Rome, this is
bad news and though the upshot is not that I am constantly
riddled with agonies my thing is often worse for I cannot get purchase on life.

7

Among the flaws that mar my sleep I harbour more than wars for I have
    friends and lacerations,
brave men and spritely women, lovers of Dylan
whose fears dovetail and though often our gentleness for our lover
is straight and incomparable,
we impose the roles that feed the other's
hankering and go on to
savage what we have made, defacing
images, our own, and thus finally
destroy the beloved trapped inside the image.
And the nerve-ends come apart and we spend
long nights separate in the same bed, turning and raunchy as if
our dreams were real for there are
few among us who are competent at being, and few who can
let our lovers be.
And some are freed by the breakdown but many at once will
lapse back into the game, projecting our
monstrous images back outside us again, where we will
deface them again and again destroy the beloved,
and there is never any end to it while we are alive.

And some move through these hard necessities
like losers for awhile, but then they
reach some kind of ease in their bodies' loving;
the agony hunger fades, they come to a
difficult rhythm together, around
their job and the kids, that allows for a
tentative joy and often for grieving together.

But mostly each man carries his lover's fate
inside him, which he fears as it stirs because if the drinks are strong
or the conversation proceeds just so it will rise up and contemptuously
destroy him, and at last when he meets the other
with his own fate trapped like a bubble inside her body
there is a baleful chemistry which draws them together for love and the kill.
And out of that horror of life

they take on the crippled roles that each has singled the
other to partner, the voluntary betrayal is
consummated and they are confirmed again
in postures of willing defeat and furious at their own fresh self-abolition
they tear strips off the other who has been their accessory.
And they walk all night in the street for the fate is still in them,
and it is a rash passer who does not see himself on the go half out of his
    mind with the need to fail and be hurt,
for these were brave men and subtle women, spritely lovers
who could not love themselves and it is
hard that we have only
one life for mostly we cannot command the courage outright to exist
and the months slip by and still we have not started,
and every year attaches itself behind and we have more to drag.

Faced with the onus of living our civilisation, here, in this time,
do we also single out leaders because they will
dishonour us, because they will diminish us?
And they act our hearts' desire for always they are
bulldozed by yankees, menaced by slant-eyed gooks and happily there is
no hope that we might come to our own
and live, with our claimed selves, at home in the difficult world.

8

I come to the square each time there is nothing and once, made calm again
by the spare vertical glory of right proportions,
watching the wind cut loose as it riffled the clouds on the skyline, framing
    the towers at noon,
catching the newsboys' raucous cry of race in the streets and the war and
    Confederation going,
smelling the air, the interminable stink of production and transport and
caught once more in the square's great hush with the shoppers, hippies,
    brokers, children, old men dozing alone by the pool and waiting,
feeling the pulse in the bodies jostling past me driving to climax and
    dollars and blood,
making my cry here quick and obscure among many in transit—not as a
lyric self in a skin but divided, spinning off many selves to attend each
    lethal yen as it passed me—thinking of
death in the city, of others' and also my own and of many born afterwards,
I saw that we are to live in the calamitous division of the world
with singleness of eye and there is
nothing I would not give to be made whole.

Hector de Saint-Denys-Garneau
you came this way and made poems out of your body,
out of the palpable void that opened
between the bones of your spine—if you weren't just
making it up, you thought,
and humbled yourself again.
But your friends could only see that you were a genius,
and humiliated by their nonchalance as they strolled through space, as if
they belonged, as if their tickets had been accepted,
you turned back and fingered the precious emptiness, feeling inside you
the small incessant gush of the cardiac lesion.
And often you left the room when the party was
reaching its climax, and you had been foremost in repartee, Garneau
and fell crouching upstairs in a sweat by the bed, sick with repentance and
stammered out holy names,
destroyed by what was quick and sexual in Montreal.
But you lasted ten years more, in a suave vertigo

assaying the void with your nerve-ends, watching your
friendships go numb, your poems, nursing
the adorable death of the Son in your own imperious cells, a man made
empty for love of God, straining to be only
an upright will in the desert, until at last the world's hypnotic
glitter was made single in the grace of renunciation.

But the kids, and the calm, and the endless parade of lethal desirable things
divide us as they pass by with clowns, the tawdry
yammering goes on inside and it yanks us here and every
whichway, we are on all fronts and forming
new precious attachments and
often they stun us till what is authentic is obliterated and heeding it or
even locating it becomes one more hangup, all that great
longing keeps banging back against the miscellaneous clobber of day to day.

And by these distractions we are saved, for there is a barren route that the
    blood knows,
and the obscure inklings of the implacable imagination declare it,
lonely among bedclothes before the light on Tuesdays;
and though I will not speak of where I have not been it is
the graveyard of many for want of the lore of emptiness,
which once was a sane thing, but now of those who begin
their lonely inward procession I
do not know a chastened handful who survive.

Catatonic exemplar,
cardiac, scrupulous, hagridden—you, Hector,
our one patrician maker, mangled spirit,
you went all out for fame and when you knew you would not survive in the
    world you turned to sainthood,
and you beat down the thought for the pride and retreated to
Sainte-Catherine, you watched your blood lap wide on the lake at sunset,
thinking of John of the Cross, patron of void, thinking of Jesus,
and you watched the ferns come shouldering up through your body, the
    brutal ferns in spring, it was all

detachment you hoped, it was
exquisite penetration, it was
fear of life, the mark of Canada.
And now across
two decades and two nations de Saint-Denys-Garneau, my blessed stricken
original, still haunted by the
space between your ribs, maker and friend and comfortless, my
lone heroic starter, out of my own wrong start I
keep my distance and praise.

The crowds gust through the square, the crowds and the refuse.
The luminous towers preside.
Of high detachment there are many counterfeits;
the world is itself, though sundry.
And I will not enter void till I come to myself
nor silence the world till I learn its lovely syllables,
the brimful square and the dusk and the war and the crowds in motion at
    evening, waiting to be construed
for they are fragile, and the tongue must be sure.

9

Here, as I sit and watch, the rusty leaves hang taut with departure.
The last few tourists pose by the Moore and snap their proof that they
    were also alive.
And what if there is no regenerative absence?
What if the void that compels us is only
a mood gone absolute?
We would have to live in the world.
What if the dreary high-rise is nothing but
banks of dreary high-rise, it does not
release the spirit by fraying its attachment,
for the excellent reason that there is no place else to go?
We would have to live in it, making our lives on earth.
Or else a man might go on day by day
in love with emptiness, dismayed each time he meets
good friends, fine buildings and grass in the acres of concrete, feeling the
city's erotic tug begin once more, perpetually
splayed alive by the play of his bungled desires,
though some do not salute the death of the body
before they have tested its life, but crippled they summon together
the fury from within, they tilt at
empire, empire, lethal adversary;
but I am one who came to
idolatry, as in a season of God,
taking my right to be from nothingness.

Across the square the crisp leaves blow in gusts, tracing
the wind's indignant lift in corners,
filling the empty pool.
People plod past through the raw air, lost in their overcoats.
I hunch down close to my chest and eat smoke.

But when the void became void I did
let go, though derelict for months
and I was easy, no longer held by its negative presence
as I was earlier disabused of many things in the world
including Canada, and came to know I still had access to them,
and I promised to honour each one of my country's failures of nerve and its
    sellouts.

To rail and flail at a dying civilisation,
to rage in imperial space, condemning
soviet bombers, american bombers—to go on saying
no to history is good.
And yet a man does well to leave that game behind, and go and find
some saner version of integrity,
although he will not reach it where he longs to, in the
vacant spaces of his mind—they are so
occupied. Better however to try.

But we are not allowed to enter God's heaven, where it is all a
drowsy beatitude, nor is God, the realm above our heads but
must grow up on earth.
Nor do we have recourse to void.
For void is not a place, nor
negation of a place.
Void is not the high cessation of the lone self's burden,
crowned with the early nostalgias;
nor is it rampant around the corner, endlessly possible.
We enter void when void no longer exists.

And best of all is finding a place to be
in the early years of a better civilisation.
For we are a conquered nation: sea to sea we bartered
everything that counts, till we have
nothing to lose but our forebears' will to lose.
Beautiful riddance!
And some will make their choice and eat imperial meat.
But many will come to themselves, for there is
no third way at last and these will
spend their lives at war, though not with
guns, not yet—with motherwit and guts, sustained
by bloody-minded reverence among the things which are,
and the long will to be in Canada.

The leaves, although they cling against the
wind do not resist their time of dying.
And I must learn to live it all again, depart again—
the storm-wracked crossing, the nervous descent, the barren wintry land,
and clearing a life in the place where I belong, re-entry
to bare familiar streets, first sight of coffee mugs,
reconnaissance of trees, of jobs done well or badly,
flashes of workday people abusing their power,
abusing their lives, hung up, sold out and
feeling their lives wrenched out of whack
by the steady brunt of the continental breakdown;
finding a place among the ones who live
on earth somehow, sustained in fits and starts
by the deep ache and presence and sometimes the joy of what is.

Freely out of its dignity the void must
supplant itself. Like God like the soul it must
surrender its ownness, like eternity it must
re-instil itself in the texture of our being here.
And though we have seen our most precious words
withdraw, like smudges of wind from a widening water-calm,
though they will not be charged with presence again in our lifetime that is
well, for now we have access to new nouns—
as water, copout, tower, body, land.

Earth, you nearest, allow me.
Green of the earth and civil grey:
within me, without me and moment by
moment allow me for to
be here is enough and earth you
strangest, you nearest, be home.

Notes

Some of the references in *Civil Elegies* are highly local. The following notes should clarify them.

1. — The Square: Nathan Phillips Square, a large plaza in front of Toronto's New City Hall, at the junction of Queen and Bay Streets.
   — The Moore, the Archer: the abstract sculpture which Henry Moore created for the Square.
   — Revell: the Finnish architect who designed the New City Hall.
   — Chartier: in 1966 Paul Chartier tried to blow up the House of Commons in Ottawa.

4. — Hector de Saint-Denys-Garneau (1912-1943): Québec's first modernist poet. There are phrases from his *Journal* in the fourth and eighth elegies.

5. — The Golden Horseshoe: a name given to the megalopolis at the western end of Lake Ontario.
   — Paul Martin: the Secretary of External Affairs under Lester Pearson.